# THE MEDIA

By Lord Loveday Ememe and available from Lulu.
The constitution and Policing
Heresy
Starfleet
The Supernatural
Creation
Deterrence
Stalking

www.lulu.com
Copyright© Lord Loveday Ememe 2012
The author asserts the moral right to be recognized as the author of this work.
ISBN: 978-1-291-33064-9

## Table of Contents

1. The information provided by the media is based on a false reality created by the uncivilized to persecute the vulnerable including the civilized.
2. The media is political and a representation of the uncivilized nature, which is unconstitutional.
3. The information provided by the media can be corrected to be based on reality as defined by the constitution without being intrusive but educational.
4. The unlawful policing of the civilized by the media
5. Author's notes
6. Author's biography
Bibliography

1. THE INFORMATION PROVIDED BY THE MEDIA IS BASED ON A FALSE REALITY CREATED BY THE UNCIVILIZED TO PERSECUTE THE VULNERABLE INCLUDING THE CIVILIZED.

The information provided by the media, which includes the internet, news broadcasts on radio and television, documentaries on radio and television are all based on a false reality created by the uncivilized to persecute the vulnerable including the civilized. The media in its current state is a demonic weapon used to create lawlessness and to undermine the constitution of this planet, the Christian principles or civil rights. The media is a representation of the uncivilized nature of the uncivilized or supernaturalism. The constitution, the Christian principles or civil rights regulates the use of supernatural powers and senses and does not allow its misuse to harm mentally or physically the civilized or to breach the peace in a civilized society. The media which is supernatural is operating completely illegally.

The use of supernatural powers and senses, supernaturalism, regardless of its purpose has an unhealthy effect on the civilized when exposed to it. When Eve was created for Adam in the Garden of Eden, Adam was protected from supernaturalism because of his civilized nature then.

In order for the media, the content and delivery of information by the media to adhere to the strict guidelines of the constitution, there should be no direct or indirect hint of supernaturalism.

It is baffling that the media, who are the principle architects of the spread of the wrong interpretation and application of the constitution, aimed at creating total anarchy and destruction in the world, regard themselves as providing the necessary checks and balances to hold politicians accountable for their actions, which is a lie. Politics is a criminal activity which the media completely supports, so what types of accountability are they after when the destructive damage has already been done by endorsing the unconstitutional practice of politics, which is really demonism.

For the media to operate legally and hold accountable the uncivilized that misuse their supernatural powers and senses it must believe in the principle of complete disestablishmentarianism, given the current state of affairs in the world today. They cannot cling on to the old values of catering to the opinion of those the constitution defines as criminals. They need to let go of demonism, the direct or indirect misuse of supernatural powers and senses.

The white race have not adjusted to the constitutional authority of the civilized like me, they have a strange interest in me, like that of a slave and a slave master or a pet, or an animal they are breeding for their consumption in the future. It is reflected in the derogatory manner or content of their conversations with me that they always initiate with the direct or indirect misuse of their supernatural powers and senses. They are aware of the importance of the law, which the civilized like me are living representations of, but they want to or are using the law illegally for their illegal agenda of spreading demonism and oppressing or dominating those different from them. They cannot comprehend or accept the instruction of the constitution that the civilized like me are commissioners of police, king of kings or lord of lords. It is a misconception to think that the reference to a king of kings or lord of lords is a reference to the supernatural. If they understand correctly the interpretation of the constitution's reference to the son of God, it means that the son or children of God can only be of a civilized nature, similar to the original nature of Adam in the Garden of Eden, before his constitution was unlawfully altered. The references to the son or children of God are a symbolic acknowledgement of the civilized constitution as the legitimate rulers of the planet and universe. It does not mean that the uncivilized are superior to the civilized, if at all, it is the opposite.

The white race regardless of appearances have a serious problem with authority or following orders. They prefer illegitimate authority figures of the uncivilized because it involves them humiliating themselves or are humiliated by the uncivilized, which makes it possible for them to accept their illegitimate authority. This is not possible with real authority figures of the civilized constitution; as a consequence they are reluctant to follow the instructions of the constitution with regard to the official implementation of the constitutional authority of the civilized. They have not figured out yet that they do not have a choice.

A supernatural or red administration involves someone else unlawfully making life or death decisions for someone else regardless of whether you are good or bad.

A civil or blue administration involves you making decisions for yourself. The right to independence or self-determination is not interfered with directly or indirectly by altering the constitutional living conditions meant for the civilized.

The bible mentions a situation that developed which highlights the dangers of supernaturalism which the current state of the media represents. The tower of babel, their curiosity got the better of them, when they collectively built a tower and were made to separate by making them speak different languages or individual rights and personal freedoms.

Whatever your views are on a market economy or the current version of capitalism, it is clear that the differences in the constitutions of the civilized and the uncivilized mean that a civilized person should not have anything less than the equivalent of one hundred million pounds to ensure the independence and peace of mind of the civilized. This should be considered a basic amount. The uncivilized should not undermine this determination by unlawfully comparing themselves to the civilized. Anything less than that will suggest that the uncivilized collectively are severely mentally impaired as a consequence of the psychological profile of a mentally fit uncivilized person established in the Garden of Eden when Adam was created, when the creator a supernatural instructed that Adam is the ruler of the planet, universe, and everything in it belonged to him.

The uncivilized, those with supernatural powers and senses, need to understand for their own security, that from when this universe was created they have never had the constitutional authority or legitimacy to govern or rule, even when they pretend to civilized, those without supernatural powers and senses. The constitution considers the actions of the uncivilized that pretend to be civilized in order to rule or govern a serious crime. When the uncivilized while pretending to be civilized make rules or govern and make decisions that adversely affects the mental or physical wellbeing of the civilized or that breaches the peace in a civilized society, they will be severely punished. The punishment will be severe, proportionate to their superhuman strengths. Although politics is illegal or unconstitutional, the uncivilized do not fall within the legal or moral definition of a man and do not have the legal right to vote.

It needs to be mentioned that politics which is supernatural, the white race's interpretation of Christianity is supernatural, and the main language the English language exported around the world is supernatural, these exports by the white race are mechanisms intent on persecuting the vulnerable or the civilized. The media are the primary method currently of exporting these supernatural mechanisms. As someone of a civilized nature and of African origin I cannot be comfortable around a white person.

The United Nations was established or created in response to the aftermath of the persecution of the Jews by the Germans, to prevent human rights violations. The Germans represent the uncivilized and the Jews represent the civilized. Although it must be said that the misuse of supernatural powers and senses by the uncivilized to harm the civilized mentally or physically is worse than the historical account or record of the persecution of the Jews by the Germans.

The constitution's direction or instruction for the indiscriminate destruction of the uncivilized is as a

consequence of the way the uncivilized collectively persecute the civilized and breach the peace in a civilized society with the misuse of their supernatural powers and senses regardless of appearances. The media is a clear evidence of the collective way the uncivilized persecute the civilized.
The only approved education or knowledge for Adam or the civilized is about the problems associated with supernaturalism.
Supernaturalism is unnatural, similar in principle to homosexuality but by far worse than that because of its extremely unhealthy effects on the civilized and its disruptive effects in a civilized society.
As I am writing this book I am under attack by what I can only refer to as thunder and lightning by the uncivilized that think that they can undermine the law or the constitutional authority of the civilized. They unsuccessfully tried to initiate personal relationships with me outside the guidelines of the constitution, the point of the attempt is for power tripping or bullying purposes, the civilized as constitutional rulers of the planet, universe, are a tempting prospect for the self-destructive uncivilized, they like to show off to their peers by challenging the sacred authority of the civilized. The massive differences mean that this type of attack is a compliment to my efforts to tell the truth about their criminal activities. Given the massive differences as a consequence of their supernatural powers and senses this type of attack makes them appear pathetic and weak. They are rebels without a cause.
The civilized as commissioners of police or rulers which is part of our constitution or nature is not subject to a specified period, it is indefinite, permanent, as ageing is not meant to be part of our constitution or make up. There are no retirements.
The unfortunate persecuted situation of the civilized is similar in principle but worse than the situation of the Jews in Nazi Germany, where their every movement was watched or scrutinized in order to have an excuse to torture them, if they cannot find anything they make one up. The circumstances of the civilized is worse because we are being watched or scrutinized supernaturally, if they cannot find anything they misuse their supernatural powers and senses to make something up to justify unprovoked attacks. According to the guidance of the constitution, the misuse of supernatural powers and senses to harm the civilized mentally or physically, directly or indirectly, and to breach the peace in a civilized society is forbidden, regardless of age, race, skin colour, gender or biological connections. It needs to be noted that the persecution of the Jews was done by those of the same race, the white race.
The media are at the forefront of the deliberate misinterpretation of the constitution's definition of work in order to persecute the civilized and undermine law and order. The constitution defines work as the use of supernatural powers and senses, which the civilized do not have and as a consequence should not be misled into going along with the new work concept developed by the uncivilized. The social security benefits are based on the illegal definition of work aimed at torturing the civilized. Although the social security benefits system is based on the wrong definition of work, it confirms in principle that the disabled are meant to have more money than the abled bodied person, it confirms the instruction of the constitution that the planet or universe and its contents belong to the civilized and not the uncivilized. The meek shall inherit the earth.
My experiences confirm that the uncivilized have no self-respect, and because of their supernatural powers and senses have no consciousness which makes them a danger to themselves and those around them. It is evident in conversations or contacts with the civilized that they always try to initiate directly or indirectly which is extremely unhealthy for the civilized. They misuse their

supernatural powers and senses to cripple the civilized, financial security, health, in order to force unhealthy contacts, while at the same time trying to make it appear voluntary.

To be a lord of the realm you have to be of a civil nature, those without supernatural powers and senses. You can commission your own police force with your own distinct colours (livery) and those wearing your colour have to be trained to your own specifications to meet your specific needs. In my case this will require those wearing my colours to be trained in order to behave or act within the guidelines of the constitution.

The uncivilized psychopaths should not consider the reaction of the civilized to their misuse of supernatural powers and senses to be fear or embarrassment but a reaction to an attack. Embarrassment implies valuing the opinion of uncivilized psychopaths. They also try to create a type of reaction from the civilized from their attacks, which says a lot about the uncivilized rather than the civilized.

The civilized as living representations of the law are the only ones authorized to grant land rights to the uncivilized if we want to, our consent cannot be forced or land taken by force without the expressed consent of the civilized. It also needs to be noted that land is in some circumstances referred to as earth.

## 2. THE MEDIA IS POLITICAL AND A REPRESENTATION OF THE UNCIVILIZED NATURE, WHICH IS UNCONSTITUTIONAL

The media as a representation of the uncivilized nature is subject to the guidelines outlined in the constitution regarding the use of supernatural powers and senses; it cannot be used to harm the civilized mentally or physically or to breach the peace in a civilized society.

This also suggests that the content and delivery should not be supernatural. When they are giving information it should not be done as if to a particular individual listening or watching because that is supernatural and extremely unhealthy for the civilized.

The collective ways the uncivilized persecute the civilized is evident with the misleading information by the media. The relationship between Adam and the creator was the foundation or where civil rights were created, the information provided and the way it was provided was done in a healthy civilized manner, which characterizes the mental state of a healthy supernatural.

The media is currently operating completely illegally or demonically, show no substance. As a civilized person who has been and continue to be persecuted by uncivilized psychopaths, my movements as a consequence have been severely restricted, I live like a political prisoner in my home. My neighbours are used as tools to cause me mental harm as supernaturalism is unhealthy, so I do not know them or socialize with them. But I am being bullied indirectly collectively by uncivilized psychopaths that want to force an unwanted relationship with my neighbours, that deliberately ignore delivery instructions and try to leave or leave ordered items at my neighbours to create false impressions, even when I have told my neighbours not to accept items on my behalf because I do not know them or want to know them. Even when I informed the police of this, they ignored my complaint, my experiences and the law confirm that the police are currently being used by demons for demonic purposes. For the police to operate demonically they have to fail to acknowledge their constitutional leaders the civilized (those without supernatural powers and senses). If they do not acknowledge the constitution's instructions that the civilized are commissioners of the metropolitan police force it means that they are operating illegally or demonically.

When in 1998/1999 I started becoming aware of the differences and the abuses I was subjected by the uncivilized collectively, not even one person tried to ease my mind, as I was going through very serious emotional turmoil, and for 10 years since then. Not even neighbours, they appeared to enjoy my pain and the feeling of having power over the vulnerable. So I do not socialize with the uncivilized I see them as a completely different species from me.

The uncivilized psychopaths while pretending to be civilized make civil rights concessions or compromises to those amongst themselves they consider to be demons or reds. The question is, under whose authority are they making these civil rights concessions or compromises? They do not have the legal authority or legal status to speak for the civilized or represent the civilized.

The media keep on misleading the civilized into believing that eating meat is okay when it is illegal. It is not just about killing animals which is bad enough but the act which encourages violence and no value for life. Even if the uncivilized can supernaturally replicate meat for consumption without killing an animal it is still unlawful because it encourages the young to have no value for life. The constitution instructs that we are meant to be vegetarians which make sense to me. It is not an aggressive act which helps the uncivilized exercise self-control.

With regard to entertainment films and music, and whether the content of some films are violent or not. It is arguable about what is the definition of violence given what is possible supernaturally, which confirms that these films really are fiction. But for the wellbeing of the uncivilized more care has to be taken with the making of films or music. The civilized are not violent naturally so it has no effect on us, but the uncivilized because of the possibility of violent behaviour given their supernatural powers and senses it is possible that it could have an adverse effect on them making them dangerous to themselves and those around them. So, although they are correct with film classifications in principle less emphasis should be placed on age but rather on whether you are civilized or uncivilized. The only problem for the civilized with films and music are the illegal recent alterations to them, making the images and voices not just living but supernatural.

The uncivilized that think they are blues or angels should know that that status is determinant on the living conditions and status of the civilized. For political reasons the uncivilized are desperately trying to take advantage of limited opportunities that I have contact with them or communicate with them to try to discredit me; according to the constitution, it is impossible. For them to succeed is for them to lose big. To undermine the civilized is to undermine law and order, which creates hell on earth.

The nightmare encountered by the civilized is the misconception that role play is friendly or the blue ideology, which presumes that the civilized want to socialize with the uncivilized. The uncivilized need to understand before making self-destructive assumptions, that if the constitutional living conditions are in place, which is possible, there really is nothing to talk about only in circumstances of companionship. This does not include the limited circumstances in the role of the civilized as rulers or commissioners of the metropolitan (civilization) police force. Conversations or contacts outside this will be interpreted by the constitution as forced illegally on the civilized, which is a type of enslavement of the civilized to the barbarism of the uncivilized, regardless of appearances.

The civilized should always have access to what we want immediately, and the process of access should not be tasking, for example food. The condition in the Garden of Eden is a blue print of how to align the conditions in a modern world to meet the standards stipulated by the constitution.

The white race supported by their creation the media have exported the misconception that it is possible for the civilized to commit crimes contrary to the guidelines of the constitution. They have also misused their supernatural powers and senses to create oppressive living conditions for the civilized to fuel the misconception, in order to discredit the civilized. They have also tried to create the misconception that the uncivilized are above the law. The law was created to regulate the use of supernatural powers and senses; the civilized are living representations of the law. The real interpretation of the law means that a criminal is a demon, to be a demon you must possess supernatural powers and senses to misuse.

They have invested a lot of time and effort and ingenuity into the systematic unlawful persecution of the civilized.

They believe that they can pretend to be a sacred civilized constitution to misuse their supernatural powers and senses to harm the civilized and get away with it, which is impossible.

Politics is a criminal activity that undermines law and order and the constitution, it is a compromise reached by uncivilized psychopaths that want to give those they consider to be demons amongst themselves the unrestricted opportunity to wreak havoc in a civilized society. It is worse than creating an opportunity for a rape and paedophilia party to govern and to impose their ideals on the public. Women and children will continue to have sleepless nights worrying about whether or not the rape and paedophilia party will gain power and govern.

Government ministers are entitled to a chauffeur driven government car, chef, gardener, maid, steward, these are civil rights meant for the civilized, if you are of an uncivilized nature you do not need these benefits and you are not entitled to them. These civil rights or benefits are on-going until the uncivilized come up with ways to do these things that are not tasking for the civilized.

Noah's Ark or a star ship is based on the principle of establishing and maintaining a police force to establish and maintain law and order, or universal peace and security. The distinction of the civil nature as commissioners of police should not be undermined in order to respect a constitutional instruction and universal peace and security. The principle is correct, but with a reverse role. The ruler or rulers and criminals have to be properly identified and a distinction made before a decision is made regarding the appropriate punishment. A crime is defined by the constitution as the misuse of supernatural powers and senses to undermine the constitutional living conditions of the civilized and to breach the peace in a civilized society.

The mistake the uncivilized make when they scheme to undermine the constitutional authority of the civilized is their lack of understanding that the existence of the differences in the civilized and the uncivilized constitutions means that the civilized are incapable of wrongdoing(sinning or hostility). They are so desperate to undermine the constitutional authority of the civilized that they want to draw the civilized into role plays for the civilized to be forced into pretending to be hostile or committing sins. The constitution is sacred and will interpret this as unprovoked attacks on the civilized, the civilized have nothing to gain from participating in role plays that undermine our constitutional authority and law and order.

The uncivilized force their way supernaturally into the lives of the civilized by sabotaging or exploiting our interests in order to unlawfully undermine our civil rights. When they unlawfully force their way into the lives of the civilized supernaturally they try to create false impressions. What reaction can they reasonably expect from the civilized, given the supernatural powers and senses of the uncivilized? It is similar to an Egyptian forcing contact with an Israelite slave during the period of Moses. What reaction should they reasonably expect from the Israelite? Or a Nazi forcing contact with a Jew in Germany during the Second World War. What reaction should they reasonably expect from the Jew? No assumptions should be made from these circumstances because it will not be a true reflection of the situation. Any assumptions made will be for the sole benefit of the oppressor or oppressors.

The uncivilized are by nature hyperactive, which is an understatement; it makes their judgements extremely dangerous when they want to plan the lives of the civilized. They will plan the lives of the civilized along the lines of the hyperactive nature of the uncivilized nature. The mental and physical limitations of the civil nature when compared to the uncivilized nature are the constitution's definition of life.

The uncivilized try to create a hostile relationship with the civilized because of their hostile nature. They unlawfully altered films and music by turning them supernatural for political purposes to undermine the constitutional authority of the civilized. The alterations have been turned into a type of media, unwelcomed and uninvited which has deviated from the trade description of the products. The purpose I believe is if the civilized continue with our interests or hobbies with these illegal alterations the uncivilized will want to interpret it as the civilized selling our souls to the devil. These are rules they have unlawfully created to undermine the legal and moral superiority of the civilized. Their actions are similar to the biblical accounts of Delilah's efforts to undermine the strength of Samson. In this case the uncivilized represent Delilah and the civilized represent Samson. Unfortunately the media's agenda from conception is to promote and maintain lawlessness and the unlawful persecution of the civilized.

The magnitude of the deliberate misinformation and encouragement of genocide by the media only confirms the collective conspiracy of the uncivilized to create unlawfully hell on earth. It makes no difference if you are good or bad. This is evident in the conspiracy by the uncivilized lead by the media to compromise the civil nature of the civilized. The trap set for them with the sacred world's natural sifting ability, is that contrary to the misconception it is impossible to compromise the civil nature of the civilized. This is because they need the consent of the civilized which is impossible to obtain. It makes no difference whether they think they have obtained the consent of the civilized, the constitution will interpret it as coercion. This is because there is nothing to gain for the civilized from the alteration of our civil nature.

The white race are very political especially when it aids their demonic culture at the expense of law and order and the constitutional authority of the civilized. They try to use black or brown people of African origin but of an uncivilized constitution to mask their persecution of the civilized like me. They need to understand that the uncivilized collectively regardless of skin colour or biological connections have more in common with each other than with the civilized. It makes no difference what their skin colour is, a black uncivilized person has more in common with a white uncivilized person, than with a black civilized person, which shows with their collective unlawful persecution of the civilized.

3. THE INFORMATION PROVIDED BY THE MEDIA CAN BE CORRECTED TO BE BASED ON REALITY AS DEFINED BY THE CONSTITUTION WITHOUT BEING INTRUSIVE BUT EDUCATIONAL.

The media as a supernatural mechanism is subject to the guidelines of the constitution, regarding the use of supernatural powers and senses in a civilized society and when in direct or indirect contact with the civilized. The media should be educational and not used as a weapon to stalk people. Law enforcement agencies will have their own way of tracking or arresting the uncivilized that commit crimes. The delivery and content of information should be based on reality and should not be supernatural. No individual should be targeted directly or indirectly supernaturally.

In the English language life spelt back to front or end to start is evil; this could sum up their self-destructive attitude to life that they are exporting worldwide, especially through the media. Regardless of your views there are strict guidelines in the constitution about the appropriate living conditions, which ensures that if someone or a group of people give up on life it should not affect others. It ensures and maintains your independence and protects the vulnerable from suicide pacts of the uncivilized psychopaths.

The uncivilized from my experiences have very serious behavioural problems whether they think they are in law enforcement or not, it is natural to the uncivilized. This means that to create or establish a legal law enforcement agency, the training programme should be tailored to seriously control their behavioural problems in order for them to have the legitimacy to assist the civilized(commissioners of the metropolitan police force) to establish and maintain law and order. They need to aspire to the qualities or characteristics of the civil constitution in order to be in law enforcement and to remain in law enforcement. Part of their training programme is to be able to identify their commanding officers the civilized as commissioners of the metropolitan police force. If they do not have the discipline or temperament to acknowledge the civilized as their commanding officers then they are too weak and do not have the discipline to be in or remain in the metropolitan police force.

Given the natural behavioural problems of the uncivilized constitution, they need to be security vetted in all aspects of employment in public service as they assist the civilized (commissioners of the metropolitan police force) in providing and maintaining universal peace and security.

I tried to listen to the radio, and found out that the Olympic games is still on in the United Kingdom, a deception supported by the media, an event not based on reality, which supports and promotes supernaturalism contrary to the constitution.

All aspects of public service including the media according to the instructions of the constitution are commissioned by the civilized as commissioners of the metropolitan police force under the strict order to provide these services in accordance with the guidelines of the constitution formulated in the Garden of Eden. Unfortunately these services, including the media, are operating illegally outside these stipulated guidelines, they are operating under a demonic culture and a complete misinterpretation of the constitution, which promotes lawlessness and the persecution of the vulnerable.

Given the obvious behavioural problems of the uncivilized constitution or nature, there should be serious security checks done before an uncivilized person can have direct or indirect contact with the civilized.

The behavioural problems of the uncivilized nature are evident in services like the ordering and delivery of goods. They have misused their supernatural powers and senses to create services that require some type of direct or indirect contact with them before having access to these goods and services, given their natural behavioural problems it is extremely hazardous for the civilized. It is quite clear that given what is possible with their supernatural powers and senses in particular the replication technology in the constitution and in science fiction films like Star Trek, there is no need to put the civilized in dangerous situations that require contact with the uncivilized every time we need goods or services.

In some circumstances the uncivilized are completely blind to their toxic nature, which is obvious to the constitution and the civilized.

Taking into account the toxic nature of the uncivilized constitution, there should be a complete overhaul of all public sector services including the media, to make sure that the measure used to determine their suitability, is its relevance and acceptability to the civilized. Timing is a very important factor in determining whether a service is provided in line with the law or to cater to the toxic nature of the uncivilized.

According to the constitution of the United Kingdom and this planet, the public sector that is meant to set the standard for the private sector is operating illegally. This includes the media, the judiciary, the police forces etc.

The uncivilized constitution or nature is a natural contaminant in a civilized society and to the civilized constitution or nature. This is the reasoning behind the ejection of Adam and Eve from the Garden of Eden once their civilized constitutions were altered, because their new constitutions the uncivilized constitution became a natural contaminant in a civilized society, the Garden of Eden.

It needs to be noted that given the delicate nature of the civil constitution, which is the reasoning behind ensuring international peace and security, it is criminally negligent for the uncivilized to misuse their supernatural powers and senses to create doubts, uncertainty or insecurity with regard to the constitutional authority of the civil constitution. To try to undermine the confidence of the civil constitution given the massive differences between the civilized and the uncivilized constitutions is a very serious crime and unconstitutionally creates hell on earth or lawlessness.

The uncivilized collectively have unlawfully conspired to criminalize the civilized constitution or civil nature of man, before I became aware of the differences in their uncivilized constitutions and my civil constitution or nature and they continued to unlawfully try to criminalize the civil constitution. They are trying unlawfully to criminalize the civil constitution in direct and indirect ways to undermine the constitutional authority of the civilized and create and maintain lawlessness which caters to their barbaric constitutions, their supernatural instincts and hyperactive natures.

The current state of affairs in the world at present, the unlawful collective persecution of the civilized by uncivilized psychopaths means that there cannot be any legal direct or indirect contact or communication with the civilized by the uncivilized. This includes the unlawful alterations to films, music, radio and television, the images and voices have been unlawfully made not just living but supernatural (media), which is political for the continued persecution of the civilized by the uncivilized and the civilized constantly at the mercy of uncivilized psychopaths.

The deliberate misinterpretation of the constitution with regard to the idea of ageing, death and life after death is a conspiracy by demons masquerading as angels to compromise unlawfully the civil nature of the civilized. The behavioural problems of the uncivilized constitution as natural contaminants in a civilized society and to the civilized constitution will suggest that their concept of life after death in relation to their delusion of paradise is not appealing to the civilized.

The blue ideology is that of self-interest, individual rights, and the problem encountered by the uncivilized deluding themselves that they are civilized and claiming their actions to be for their own self-interest under the blue ideology is that they are not really civilized and their interests are destructive because they are generated by their hyperactive natures and supernatural instincts. The self-interest of the civilized is different; it has the added effect of providing universal peace and security. The self-interest of the civilized is generated by our civilized nature. The civilized are not naturally political. The white race are extremely political and sabotage every contact or communication with the civilized for their political agenda, which is unconstitutional. Politics is unconstitutional, it is a mechanism developed by the white race to undermine law and order. Politics is a battle cry to rise up against an established order. The civilized are naturally incapable of participating in it, also it is meant as an attack on the civilized.

The dramatics or toxicity surrounding governing is as a consequence of the uncivilized governing while pretending to be civilized and catering to their hyperactive natures and supernatural instincts. The current practice of the uncivilized psychopaths linking the prosperity of a nation or the world to the stock market is a mechanism created by the uncivilized to make the vulnerable live in fear which caters to their sadistic natures and confirms their mental state as being severely mentally unstable. They are a danger to themselves and those around them. This also confirms the threat the white race poses to the security of the universe.

In order for the uncivilized psychopaths to understand better the magnitude of their actions, they need to understand that if it is impossible while being their true constitution to play games or joke or socialize with the civilized, their abusive practices which has a harmful effect on the civilized will be categorized as attacks. And when they pretend to be civilized their actions are still guided by their hyperactive natures and supernatural instincts. This is why the constitution does not acknowledge the possibility of the civilized and the uncivilized being able to socialize or joke or play game with each other. This is why the relationship between the civilized and the uncivilized are governed by strict guidelines in the constitution. The guidelines of the constitution regarding the relationship between the civilized and uncivilized include the immediate official confirmation of the civilized as rulers or commissioners of the metropolitan police force. The uncivilized are natural contaminants in a civilized society and to the civilized, and as a consequence their actions must be regulated. This is also why they are not allowed to govern or make rules.

The uncivilized collectively are responsible for the unlawful conditions which breeds the constant persecution of the civilized, they collectively like the problems associated with real lawlessness, regardless of appearances. It is very evident in the deliberate avoidance of a reasonable solution to a problem; rather they opt for a solution which breeds problems in the future.

The uncivilized collectively regardless of appearance create horrific desperate living conditions in the lives of the vulnerable including the civilized, in order to force their way into your live illegally supernaturally to power trip and insulting your intelligence in the process.

As a civilized person who has experienced the extremely toxic nature of the uncivilized collectively and continues to experience their repulsive barbaric behavioural problems, which are extremely toxic to the civilized, I am annoyed at the unlawful supernatural alterations to my interests, like films, music, novels that expose me to unwanted dangerous indirect personal contact with the uncivilized. I honestly do not like the uncivilized they are natural contaminants to the civilized and in a civilized society. My dislike of them is similar to a natural dislike of a tornado, hurricane, thunder storms, they are natural disasters.

The reasoning behind immigration legislations is not dissimilar to that of the real constitution, any threats to public health, financial stability, and public order are not granted entry into the United Kingdom, which is similar to the Christian principles determination of the uncivilized as contaminants in a civilized society or to the civilized. The uncivilized are a threat to public order, public health and the financial stability (the deliberate creation of famine supernaturally), in a civilized society with the possible misuse of their supernatural powers and senses. Direct or indirect supernaturalism is unhealthy to the civilized and disorderly in a civilized society.

The uncivilized collectively have created the breeding ground for the continuous persecution of the civilized and the vulnerable, in some cases it is triggered by the lack of consciousness associated with their supernatural powers and senses, which makes them a danger to themselves and those around them. Given the simplicity of life, there are a lot of pointless harmful dramatics by the uncivilized. As someone of a civilized nature and because the uncivilized are natural contaminants to the civilized and in a civilized society, I cannot accept or acknowledge any relationships with them outside that stipulated by the constitution. Any relationships with them outside that stipulated by the constitution will be as a resulted of the misuse of their supernatural powers and senses to force it.

The uncivilized have unlawfully created a culture that makes them dominate or oppress the vulnerable including the civilized, countries that have nuclear weapons that are a serious threat to the existence of the planet are considered to be super powers and are always right. They use the threat of the use of their weapons to dominate or oppress weaker countries that do not have nuclear weapons; they always use the threat of their weapons to get their way even when they are wrong. It is a ploy by the uncivilized collectively that want to oppress or dominate the vulnerable, they use the threat of their supernatural powers and senses to get their way even when they are wrong, the threat of their supernatural powers and senses means that they are always right even when they are wrong with their relationship with the vulnerable including the civilized, contrary to the guidance of the constitution. This culture of the strong dominating and oppressing the weak has been encouraged and championed by the media.

According to the constitution with regard to serious issues concerning law and order which are linked to the civil rights of the civilized, communications to the civilized in riddles or in a confusing manner that deliberately creates false impressions about the intellect of the civil constitution is a serious crime. To make things confusing or deliberately tasking or difficult is aimed at catering to the hyperactive nature of the uncivilized which is disorderly and an attack on the civil constitution. A civilized society and the civilized should not be subjected to disorderly activities or enslaved to the barbarism of the uncivilized in order to cater to their hyperactive natures.

When I was unlawfully taken to a mental health unit by the uncivilized conspiring to undermine my constitutional authority and hiding the differences in their uncivilized constitutions and my civilized nature and interpreting my claims that there are differences as symptoms of a severe mental disorder, I observed that the activities and care are tailored for the uncivilized because of their hyperactive constitutions.

Houses are built deliberately in the United Kingdom to need constant repair assisted by bad weather generated by the misuse of supernatural powers and senses; this creates what will be interpreted as social activities for demons. The current unlawful system of government, the political system has been deliberately created as social activities for demons that will always be in need of constant repair. These activities are based on the opportunity for demons to bug those that are different from them. It is strange that demons succeeded in colonizing the world, regardless of appearances and after an empty symbolism of independence.

The illegal alterations made to my interests like films and music which puts me in direct contact with supernatural is unhealthy, hazardous, unwanted and always instigates unlawful interference in my life. These personal interests of mine have been unlawfully turned into an unwanted personal type of media service which puts me in constant danger given the harmful effects of supernaturalism on the civilized. The uncivilized psychopaths think that the civilized will get used to it which is wrong, they mistake the non-aggressive nature of the civil constitution as acceptance or getting used to something that is dangerous and unhealthy.

For some strange reason probably from the after effects of colonialism which affected the natural development of countries not part of the west or big economic powers, you cannot survive in those countries if you are not supernatural or dependent on a supernatural. There has been no provision made or preparation for those of the civilized constitutions. In countries like the west where it is possible you will be relegated to the disabled category. This is because of the uncivilized pretending to be civilized and denying the real civilized any chance of survival contrary to the guidance of the constitution.

The uncivilized misuse their supernatural powers and senses to plan the lives of the civilized to have unnecessary contact with them as if a toxic situation for the civilized is normal.

The illegal alterations to films and music interests built up for years before the unlawful alterations are used to force unhealthy contact with the uncivilized which creates false impressions, and the uncivilized that for some strange reason are impressionable think it is okay to force contact with the civilized and expose us to the unhealthy phenomenon of supernaturalism. These illegal alterations to films and music have turned them into dangerous types of media for political purposes that promote the interest of the uncivilized at the expense of the physical and mental wellbeing of the civilized.

The uncivilized psychopaths have deliberately crippled me financially and have been supernaturally causing damages to my property; these are there ideas of punishment for falling short of their demonic laws that has no resemblance to the real constitution. These punishments are for actions that I am meant to have done while having no contact with anyone, because I have refused contact with the uncivilized since becoming aware of the differences they were hiding while at the same time causing me mental and physical abuse. The punishments are for actions that have been done because of the unwanted supernatural interactions they have initiated by altering my interests. Because of my civilized nature I will always be a symbol of what demons are fighting against which makes life for me hell, contrary to the guidance of the constitution.

I am not making anything up with regard to the impossibility of the civilized and the uncivilized being able to naturally play games together, socialize or joke with each other. This is confirmed in the class or social structure in the United Kingdom, the nobles or civilized do not socialize, joke or plays games with the working class or the uncivilized. The principle of the distinction was right; the reason for the class war was because those claiming to be civilized or nobles were uncivilized with supernatural powers and senses. The United Kingdom's constitution is the Christian principles or the civil constitution of man, the social or class structure is meant to be an education on the constitutional authority of the civilized that are living representations of the law, the law that is meant to regulate the use of supernatural powers and senses in order to establish and maintain order.

The white race's professed Christian ideals or respect for the law was meant as a weapon to dominate those different from them, for purposes the constitution will interpret as a demonic agenda. They have been faced with someone of a civilized constitution, which is a symbolic embodiment of the Christian ideals, for years, I, and they have been constantly trying to undermine or compromise my civil rights.

Rather than correct the unlawful indirect supernatural governments in the world representing the demonic agenda, they have extended the illegal supernatural governments to the unlawfully altered former types of entertainment, films, music, novels to become illegal supernatural governments and a new type of media service that are unhealthy for the civilized and which persecutes the civilized. The marriage vows performed in Christian ceremonies requiring the woman to honour and obey the man, are not vows meant for an uncivilized woman and an uncivilized man but between a supernatural woman and a civilized man. It simply means that the supernatural should respect the civil rights of the civilized. It was intended as an education for the uncivilized women that want to be companions of the civilized man (ruler or commissioner of police).

The attitude of the uncivilized championed by the white race through the media which is driving the world completely insane can be summarized by a title of one of William Shakespeare's book as much ado about nothing.

The current practice or interpretation of love, socializing, companionship, success, family is only compatible with the uncivilized constitution.

Trading could have been a concept developed to establish an orderly way to access goods and services, but whatever the original intention it has evolved into a barbaric or uncivilized practice because of the unnecessary requirement to have direct or indirect contact with the uncivilized which is extremely hazardous for the civilized. It also gives an unfair advantage to the uncivilized with regard to access to money, although money and contractual agreements can only be had or entered into by the civilized. The uncivilized while pretending to be civilized have made having money impossible for the civilized, unless it is direct or indirect hand outs or charity, which means that unlawfully the civilized are required to be dependent on the goodwill of uncivilized psychopaths, which compromises our constitutional role as commissioners of police or rulers.

The uncivilized, when they develop emotional entanglements want to dominate or oppress you, to achieve that they need to dent your confidence. They rely on direct or indirect force to get their way, developed from how they are naturally and how they are amongst their type. The civilized like me have nothing to gain from denting your confidence because we do not naturally rely on force to get what we want.

In conclusion the revelation of the differences and the creation of the supernatural and the natural, the civilized and the uncivilized come into this world the same way, the distinction of the civil constitution or natural as being born of God and in God's image, the civilized confirmed as rulers by the constitution, one can conclude that the civilized are Gods. So is Adam God? Yes. This means that in the interest of justice the illegal alterations made to Adam's original civil constitution should be corrected, immediately. He is born of God, which means that his original constitution was the civil constitution, which should not be altered. It was illegally altered by the collective conspiracy of the uncivilized in order to undermine his constitutional authority.

Adam and Jesus Christ have been depicted as being of the white race (pink skins); their subsequent downfall was instigated or done by those of the same race, which confirms the attitude of the white race to real law and order. This confirms that the white race (pink skins) are a serious threat to the security of this planet.

# 4. THE UNLAWFUL POLICING OF THE CIVILIZED BY THE MEDIA

The media is supernatural; the uncivilized have created a false impression that it is okay to police the civilized supernaturally. It is wrong to police the civilized supernaturally even when they think that they are trying to help. In law enforcement in the United Kingdom, if there is a suspect of a crime or when a crime is in progress, and a police officer is aware of the situation they will have to call for the firearms unit to deal with the situation when guns are being used. This is relevant when supernatural powers and senses are being used to commit crimes by the uncivilized, this will require the intervention of supernatural police officers to police the situation.

In the United Kingdom, in law enforcement, when trying to arrest or question a suspect for purposes of policing, a police officer is required to use reasonable force to approach or apprehend the suspect.

A supernatural police officer that has any sort of contact with the civilized, given the massive differences in the civilized constitution and the uncivilized constitution, will mean that the contact will never be interpreted as reasonable force. This is important to note, because according to the guidance of the real constitution, the bible or the civil constitution of man, crimes can only be committed by the misuse of supernatural powers and senses. This means that real crimes can only be committed by the uncivilized with the misuse of their supernatural powers and senses.

The purpose of the law is to make everyone, the civilized, the uncivilized, all creatures great and small, feel special and protected from abuse.

It is your constitution that determines if you are an infant, if you are male or female, if you are supernatural or a king or ruler.

To cater to the needs of the civilized, which includes financial security or ease of access of goods and services, similar in principle to disability access to buildings or services, security of the civilized by establishing a police force to police the uncivilized, to acknowledge correctly officially the constitutional role of the civilized, the other civil rights of the civilized, the side effect will be the creation of heaven on earth.

The references to Jesus Christ as the son of God, with supernatural powers and senses, could be a reference to Lord Adam in his unlawfully altered state, which must be corrected to ensure universal peace and security.

In the bible, romans 12:19, vengeance is mine says the Lord, actually means the civil constitution and not the supernatural constitution as Lord for the purposes of law enforcement. Contrary to the misconception does not give permission to the uncivilized or supernatural to take matters into their own hands, to retaliate on behalf of anyone or themselves but that action must be taken legally against criminals under the constitutional authority of the civilized as law lords.

The constitution considers the civil nature a living sacrifice and considers any additional sacrifices forced on the civilized by the uncivilized an abomination.

The civilized are naturally strong willed because of the unhealthy effects of lawlessness on the civil constitution, as a consequences the lives of the civilized are being manipulated supernaturally by the uncivilized for political purposes. In most cases to be able to manipulate the lives of the civilized supernaturally for political purposes, the civilized must have to be crippled financially or our movements restricted. This enables the uncivilized to continue with their unlawful creation of hell on earth.

Antidisestablishmentarianism is a principle that advocates the preservation or continuation of an already established system of government. Unfortunately because of the unlawful overthrow of Lord Adam, the wrong system of government was unlawfully established and not the intended system of government.

The salaries and benefits of top government ministers are more than those of junior ministers given the differences in the constitutions of the civilized and the uncivilized and the current version of capitalism. This creates the necessary balance given the limited capacity of the civil constitution with regard to the use of supernatural powers to access goods and services. The higher salaries are meant for the civilized and the constitution has made the determination that the civil constitution gives more as a living sacrifice for peace and security.

The uncivilized are aware of the importance of the constitutional role of the civil constitution only if they can pretend to be civilized and attain to the position themselves unlawfully to dominate each other at the expense of international peace and security and at the expense of the mental and wellbeing of the civilized and vulnerable.

Unfortunately this exposes the demonic practices of the white race and their real attitudes to real law and order. As a consequence, if Lord Adam's civil constitution and constitutional authority are restored as they are required by law to do, his life, health will constantly be in danger by supernatural meddling by the white race. This will make life for him a living hell unlawfully, as he has been depicted as of the white race and the uncivilized white people have not yet mastered the emotion of enthusiasm and their constant emotional need to rebel against the law, their toxic need to constantly dominate or oppress those different from them.

In an episode of star trek the next generation, where no one has gone before, it revealed the horrors of making somebody's thoughts come to life, the impossibility of life under those circumstances. This is worse than what the uncivilized have been unlawfully doing to me for years with the misuse of their supernatural powers and senses including unlawfully trying to create an unlawful, unhealthy, unwanted supernatural relationship.

The uncivilized wrongly believe that certain processes and procedures including application processes are civilized because they pretend to be civilized during these processes, they are in fact supernatural processes and harmful to the civilized. They are based on a serious deception or lie and in most cases unnecessary and social activities for the uncivilized. These social activities are lawless social activities and harmful to the civilized.

When the uncivilized are being rejected because of the harmful effects of their lawless social activities on the health or life of the civilized, they take it personally and it becomes a challenge to them to force these harmful lawless social activities on the civilized. These activities are lawless social functioning.

The current unlawful system of government supernaturalism including politics is a compromise to cater to the hostile nature of the supernatural which defeats the purpose behind the creation of the law.

The lives of the civilized are plagued with the uncivilized trying to create dramatic effects with every situation because of the unique nature of the civilized constitution. Dramatic effects work with the element of surprise which is impossible with the uncivilized constitution, so they choose to experience this fantasy vicariously through the civilized at the expense of our physical and mental wellbeing. This makes life completely impossible for the civilized.

The civilized as law lords do not get involved in individual cases but judicially review the legality of a system of government or systems of government, and instruct or direct accordingly.

The white race are fascinated or obsessed with horror films and the emotion it generates, they see the civilized as perfect test subjects for this obsession. These practices or obsession violates the civil rights of the civilized. The unlawful interference with or restrictions of the civil rights of the civilized including financial insecurities help enable the uncivilized to indulge their fantasies or obsession at the expense of the physical and mental wellbeing of the civilized.

The uncivilized should be aware, whether they consider themselves to be angels, demons or gods, anything short of the complete change of the lawless system makes them criminals collectively with very serious consequences. The lawless system is as a result of the collective agreement of the uncivilized regardless of an appearance that is why the constitution instructs the indiscriminate destruction of the uncivilized. The lawless system in place means that it is not currently unlawful unfortunately to kill rape or harm the uncivilized mentally or physically. Knowing their fate the uncivilized have unlawfully tried to include the civilized in the sentence or judgment on the uncivilized constitution. They claim by their interpretation of the bible or constitution that death and illness are inevitable for all, as part of God's dissatisfaction. It needs to be noted that the reference to God by them is the supernatural God. This is inaccurate; the current problems are as a consequence of the law in operation indiscriminately destroying the uncivilized, which is reversible when the lawless system is changed. The uncivilized are collectively making caricatures of the constitutional role of the civilized as law lords which undermines law and order and the civil constitution.

The civil constitution or civil administration or the law represents heaven or paradise, while the uncivilized constitution or uncivilized administration represents lawlessness or hell.

I believe that word president used to identify a head of state was derived or developed from the word precedent, a legal term in reference to an act or instance that may be used as an example in dealing with subsequent similar instances. This is used to confirm that the original decision in the Garden of Eden confirming the civil constitution and not the uncivilized constitution as ruler or law lord is correct. The constitution or bible expressly forbids the uncivilized from pretending to civilized for the purpose of ruling especially when it denies the civilized the constitutional role meant for the civilized, law lords.

The contents of my law books could be an indication of a writer that is insane as the medical professionals suggest or an indication of a sane writer in an insane world.

The civil constitution according to the constitution is the right qualification to be ruler or law lord. To be a ruler or law lord you must be born or created civilized.

From my past and continuous experiences of the uncivilized constitution, it is impossible to have personal relationships with them, when they have demonstrated that their attitude towards you is dependent on which unlawful political party is in government. Whether a blue or red political party is in government will determine whether you will be abused indirectly supernaturally by the uncivilized, which is their idea of blue or whether you will be abused directly supernaturally, which is their idea of red. Either way the plan is to make the lives of those different from them revolve around constant abuses unlawfully by the uncivilized. This includes the misuse their supernatural powers and senses to set up or frame the civilized. So it will be reasonable to conclude given the nature of the civil constitution that any contact with the uncivilized is going to result in mental or physical harm.

The decisions, actions, judgements of the uncivilized are toxic to the civilized and in a civilized society. This means that they need to be guided by the law under the leadership of the civilized as law lords. Given the obvious threat the uncivilized are to the security of the universe and the security of the civilized and vulnerable, which has been demonstrated by their actions, the

constitution sees nothing wrong in the total destruction of the uncivilized.
The history of the white race shows their persecutory nature, they always strip away unlawfully the self-respect and dignity of those different from them. Lord Adam depicted as white, who because of his civilized nature which was different from their uncivilized constitutions, his self-respect and dignity had been stripped away from him. It is also possible that Lord Adam was resurrected in the form of Jesus Christ, in his unlawfully altered state as an uncivilized man, rather than cure him by restoring him to his original civilized nature, he was unlawfully killed. The demonic characteristic of the white race is a curse not for being descendants of Lord Adam but because of what was done to him by them. The only threats to the vulnerable or the civilized and the world are the uncivilized. Given the cursed status of the white race, any direct or indirect contact with races different from them will contaminate or infect other races with lawlessness or supernaturalism. They need to get their own house in order before initiating unnecessary contact with other races.

There is a legislation in the United Kingdom called the Equality Act, although unlawfully made by the uncivilized pretending to be civilized, the legislation requires reasonable adjustments to be made to public premises to enable access for the disabled to goods and services, and it has to done to accommodate the specific requirements of different disabilities, in order not to discriminate. This requirement is because of the differences generated by the different disabilities. Although the civilized are not disabled, the real constitution requires reasonable adjustments to be made, so that the civilized can access goods and services, like healthcare, information, etcetera in order to meet the constitutional living conditions meant for the civil constitution. To be able to achieve this will have the added effect of providing universal peace and security.

Lord Adam was hung out to dry by the uncivilized that thought that they could go it alone, without a proper understanding of the extreme importance of the constitutional role of the civil constitution. The civil constitution or the law is vital to the existence of those amongst the uncivilized that consider themselves to be angels or gods. For any civilization or government to operate the correct way the civilized must assume our official role as law lords with the rights, benefits or privileges that come with it.

There are two types of love, the right type that I will refer to as angelic love which put simply is law and order, and there is the wrong type of love practiced in the world today that I will refer to as demonic uncivilized love.

The uncivilized are the weakest link, preventing the right or correct type of peace keeping force being created.

A business like or professional attitude with regard to the relationship between the civilized and the uncivilized, requiring complying with the guidelines of the real constitution is the true meaning of love.

The media is meant to be a tool or aid for the civil constitution without undermining the dignity or integrity of the civil constitution. Unfortunately it is a demonic tool used to persecute those it is meant to assist because it is based on a false demonic reality created by the uncivilized to cater to their sadistic constitutions. It was not meant to be used to give the civilized an unwanted power of premonitions. Premonitions or fortune telling are only important in a demonic world that unlawfully persecutes the vulnerable. The media should stop blaming the victims of their demonic persecutory practices of any wrongdoing.

The white supernaturals responsible for lawlessness including the unlawful undermining of the constitutional authority of Lord Adam, try to use black supernaturals to undermine the constitutional authority of the black civilized.

The only relevance of God or religion in our lives is the law, the civilized as living representations of the law are as a consequence referred to as law lords.

My objective assessment of the white race is accurate although the history of the white race could have been deliberately orchestrated this way for educational purposes. If that is the case I disagree with the method, because I do not believe that life forms should be created solely for this purpose. Given the potential dangers of supernatural powers and senses it is right that the actions of the uncivilized are regulated or supervised. Also the proceeds of supernatural powers and senses or things created must be monitored for the purposes of law and order in the same way as the principle of taxation because the natural resources in a civilized society could be disrupted by the uncivilized with their supernatural powers and senses because they have an alternative source of something similar to income.

There is a difference between providing services in a civilized manner for the civilized and vulnerable and the uncivilized pretending unlawfully to be civilized unnecessarily to provide these services. The uncivilized have natural behavioural problems that will put the health and lives of the vulnerable including the civilized in constant danger when accessing these services. The references to bureaucratic red tape really mean the uncivilized exploiting the needs of the vulnerable to create social activities for themselves by making access to services unnecessarily difficult. Given the supernatural nature of the uncivilized and their need for hyper activities, some wrongly believe that they are helping the vulnerable or the civilized or those different from them by trying to force these lawless hyper social activities on us when they are not compatible with our different constitution. The uncivilized have very toxic temperaments and consider a justified refusal of their lawless advances as a challenge, and will want to force these harmful lawless social activities on those different from them. They go as far as trying to misuse their supernatural powers and senses to compromise the civil constitution or to stain the characters of the civilized in order to force their lawless social activities on the civilized. Any direct or indirect contact with the civilized by the uncivilized is for this purpose that has been my experience with them so far.

According to the constitution a curse is self-inflicted, when the uncivilized conspire to undermine the constitutional authority of the civilized. The uncivilized constitution is naturally lawless and has to behave appropriately to be law abiding. This means that it is self-defeating for the uncivilized to behave inappropriately as a joke or game because it is similar to a recovering alcoholic drinking alcohol as a joke or game it will most likely get out of control, which will be a serious threat to universal peace and security. The uncivilized because of their power tripping nature like to create false impressions that they are king makers, which is inaccurate, to be a law lord is a birth right; this means that you must be born or created civilized to be a law lord. It is as silly as a pear tree claiming to be responsible for the creation of an apple. To create a false impression like this is to make unlawfully the constitutional role of the civilized as law lords political, which defeats or compromises the role of a law lord and the requirement for a law lord not to be beholden to anyone. As someone of a civilized constitution who is by right a law lord, if the uncivilized try to manipulate this right for political purposes as if appointing me to a position that is already mine, I will not accept the appointment.

In the United Kingdom members of parliament have immunity from prosecution for things done in parliament while carrying out their duties as members of parliament. Although their constitutions are supernatural, the immunity is an education about the rights of the civilized. The civilized are not allowed to be harmed by the uncivilized under any circumstance especially in our ministerial role as law lords.

The civilized are by nature law lords (commissioner of police and Supreme Court judge), this is a position the uncivilized aspire to, the salaries for a commissioner of police is about £ 260,000 per annum and the salary of a Supreme Court judge is about £ 230,000 per annum. If you add both it is about £ 500,000 per annum. The undermining of these entitlements meant for the civilized as real law lords is a conspiracy by the uncivilized collectively to incorporate the civilized into their demonic, unnatural, homosexual practices. The term law lord is used to differentiate the civilized from the uncivilized.

Homosexuality or supernaturalism is evident everywhere because of lawlessness, the alterations to films, music, shops on every road or street because of what they sell. It is also evident in supermarkets, schools, nurseries for children, similar to the biblical accounts of Sodom and Gomorrah.

From my experiences which are also confirmed in the bible the uncivilized like to be worshipped especially by those different from them. They will go as far as creating problems in the lives of those different from them so that they appear needed. Even if you try to avoid them they misuse their supernatural powers and senses to force direct or indirect contact with them by sabotaging your interests in things like films or music to force unwanted unhealthy supernatural contact. The purpose regardless of appearances is to oppress or dominate the vulnerable, they like to be worshipped. They like to feel superior as has been evidenced by the antics of supernatural celebrities masquerading as civilized. They instigate or create problems in your life to make you dependent on the unhealthy unlawful intrusion. I like to watch films and listen to music but not in this unlawfully altered state. I remember when some years ago I had a home visit from a doctor and I asked the doctor about alterations I was seeing on television while the television was still on and his answer implied that I was hallucinating that there were no alterations. I asked him about the alterations because I found them extremely unhealthy. The uncivilized like to initiate or force unlawful contact with those different from them especially the civilized because they like being worshipped, they like to have the power of life and death, wealth or poverty or destitution over those different from them especially the civilized. This problem is acute with those different from them that they have developed unlawful emotional entanglements with. You are treated like their toy to interfere with unlawfully, planning lawless social activities supernaturally, although they try to make it appear not to be supernatural, which highlights their severe mental retardation in matters of law and order or lawful social activities.

These uncivilized psychopaths think that because they can cure the civilized after making the civilized ill mentally or physically that it is alright to harm the civilized contrary to the guidance of the constitution. When the uncivilized get emotionally entangled with the civilized whether it is their idea of love or hate, like or dislike, it is completely toxic to civilized. Being aware of their natural repulsion to the civilized they try to make you believe that you are doing something wrong in the sense of sin or crime to force themselves on the civilized when the constitution has made it clear that the differences mean that the civilized are incapable of wrongdoing. These are the reasons the constitution has instructed that the actions of the uncivilized must be regulated by law and not the civilized as they have unlawfully led us to believe by the unlawful deliberate misinterpretation of the constitution. It is strange that these legislations they keep unlawfully making do not recognize the uncivilized constitution as falling within its definition of a man or woman, which means that when they initiate contact with the civilized under these legislations they are breaking the law. These legislations implied or expressed envisage that in all circumstances involving interaction between two or more people that they must be civilized without supernatural powers and senses. This suggests that it is only the real constitution, the Christian principles or the civil constitution of man that can acknowledge their existence with the condition that the civilized be acknowledged officially as law lords with the rights and privileges as instructed by the constitution. The uncivilized are too self-destructive to obey.

Although the concept of trading as a means of accessing goods and services can be improved upon to a more civilized method, it is an orderly method of accessing goods and services. The problem is what are being sold, products and services that breaches the real constitution's health and safety guidelines. These unlawful products and services help to undermine or corrupt the educational process of the civilized. These practices undermine the delicate development of the young supernatural. The stock market concept and its link to the prosperity of many countries given what is really possible is evidence of serious madness.

The media although based on a supernatural concept because of its intrusive nature, it was meant to operate under a civilized principle without the use of supernatural powers and senses, for health and safety purposes. Even if operated by the uncivilized it should be done without the use of supernatural powers and senses, in order not to intrude upon the privacy of the civilized. Supernaturalism is unhealthy and unlawful in a civilized society and harmful to the civil constitution. As a lord law I am sure that the Christian principles or the civil constitution of man is the correct constitution of this planet given the differences. Despite the deception of the uncivilized with their misleading interpretation of the constitution, the real constitution has envisaged every possible situation given the differences and has regulations in place to deal with every situation. The uncivilized like disruptive prisoners have been misleading about the correct identification, interpretation and application of the constitution because they want to continue with their disruptive behaviour at the expense of universal peace and security.

The civil constitution has a sacred objectivity or sacred impartiality with regard to law and order, because we have nothing to gain from lawlessness, we have a natural allergic reaction to real lawlessness.

These uncivilized psychopaths misuse their supernatural powers and senses to make the civilized live from hand to mouth for political purposes, they like to pretend to be civilized to create the impression that they are blessed and the civilized are not. When the truth is that the moral standing of the uncivilized is at the pleasure of the civilized. This unlawful hand to mouth principle developed by the uncivilized is responsible for the unlawful system of government in the United Kingdom and the world, it is also responsible for the unlawful alterations to films, music, television and radio. These power tripping unlawful practices of the uncivilized cater to their hostile sadistic constitutions. These unlawful alterations are meant to make the vulnerable including the civilized dependent on the unlawful unhealthy phenomenon of supernaturalism.

Familiarity associated with supernatural powers and senses is used unlawfully through the media to undermine the civil rights of the civilized. Familiarity or supernaturalism as jokes and games are serious attempts by the uncivilized to undermine the constitutional authority or civil rights of the civilized. The constitution considers the unlawful attempts of the uncivilized to try to test the morality of the civilized an abomination and treasonous .These unlawful attempts are aimed at undermining the determination of the constitution that the morality of the civil constitution is

infallible. If there appears to any problems with the behaviour of the civilized, the source will be traced back to the misuse of supernatural powers and senses by the uncivilized.
Identity cards or passports or the registration of citizens are ways of distinguishing the civilized from the uncivilized and limit the opportunity for the uncivilized to misuse their supernatural powers and senses directly or indirectly to harm the civilized.
Since the unlawful overthrow of Lord Adam in the Garden of Eden by the unlawful conspiracy of the uncivilized, any subsequent direct or indirect contact with the uncivilized leads to the loss of self-respect and dignity of those different from them including animals. If the lives of the civilized appear chaotic or disorganized it as a consequence of direct or indirect supernaturalism or lawlessness.
The media does not represent the interest of the civilized and they do not speak for civilized. The media represents the interest of lawlessness or supernaturalism and they speak for lawlessness or supernaturalism. A new media concept developed by the uncivilized to continue with the unlawful persecution of the vulnerable in other ways is the unlawful alterations of films, music, novels, television and radio. These unlawful alterations are similar but worse than the alterations done to a television broadcast in a film called the game. The alterations were done to a television broadcast in the house of the main character played by an actor, Michael Douglas. The attack was successful because of the collective conspiracy of those that were meant to be his family and friends. These unlawful attacks drove him mad which eventually led to him to attempt taking his life, a suicide attempt. Supernaturalism or the uncivilized constitutions are not recognized in the definition of a game. The uncivilized constitution is not recognized in the United Kingdom's legislations definition of family.
The uncivilized like to make the civilized live our lives worried or stressed out about one thing or another and the sacrificial nature of the civilized constitution gives them the opportunity to do that. It is naturally impossible for the civilized and the uncivilized to play games, joke or socialize together because of the differences, whether the uncivilized pretend to be civilized or not. The film the game is an example of the madness of the uncivilized and their demonic concept of the end justifying the means. This demonic concept convinces them that interfering with your interests or things you normally do including your financial security, rights, privileges so that their restoration will give you enormous relief. All this supernatural dramatics are for a few minutes feeling of relief.
The idea or concept of entertainment is to provide a type of escapism from the harsh realities of life, which the unlawful intrusive alterations have ended. These alterations do not have the same effect on the uncivilized as they have on the civilized. It also provides an insight into the reasoning behind their unlawful version of heaven or paradise, which is different from the civilized version.
Every time the uncivilized have direct or indirect contact with the civilized, your health, life, wealth, freedom are on the line, in jeopardy. Are the uncivilized snakes as the snake in the Garden of Eden? Yes they are, especially their instincts. This method holds your attention as they are violently attention seeking.
The uncivilized bank on intimidation with the use of their supernatural powers and senses to force the vulnerable including the civilized to accept vicious unlawful attacks on us as jokes and games. For the purposes of socializing, joking and playing games the civilized and the uncivilized are not compatible. To try to force it in direct or indirect ways will result in lawlessness and mental and physical harm to the civilized. This is the reason that there are strict guidelines in the real constitution that governs interaction between the civilized and the uncivilized.
Whether the uncivilized pretend to be civilized or not they are not civilized for the purposes of law

and order.

There is an American drama series called heroes, there is a girl character in heroes who can sustain any type of injury fatal or not and still recover from the injuries. There was a male character in heroes that was part of a gang that attacked this girl character, after the incident the girl was driving a car and this male character was in the passenger seat, she drove the car deliberately into a wall because she knew that she will quickly recover from any injuries but he will not. The point here in relation to the uncivilized is that they have created certain activities that are supernatural social activities although they pretend to be civilized during these activities. These activities include interviews, applications processes etc. which they believe are governed by legislations in the United Kingdom. When the uncivilized subject each other to these activities and pretend to be civilized in the process they get away with it because neither party is recognized by the legislations and it is considered play acting. When a civilized person is forced into these activities with the uncivilized the legislation becomes operational because it recognizes the civil constitution and will consider or interpret the actions of the uncivilized as unlawful because it will not recognize the uncivilized constitution. It will interpret the actions of the uncivilized as fraudulent regardless of their misguided intention. These legislations are warnings to the uncivilized not to force the civilized directly or indirectly into these supernatural lawless social activities. The uncivilized try to manipulate the lives of the civilized to give these supernatural lawless social activities legitimacy. It will not work because the sacred protection of the civil constitution is infallible. The attempts at manipulating the lives of the civilized for these purposes are very severe unlawful supernatural attacks on the civilized by the uncivilized.

The uncivilized are not allowed to make rules or laws because they set out to make laws that will be impossible for people to meet up to the standard expected of them. And they make laws that deceive people into believing that a regulated practice or practices by these laws are lawful when they are not.

When the uncivilized psychopaths lose the moral or legal justification or argument for their demonic practices they try to fall back on their emotional entanglements with the victims of their persecutory practices, the civilized. These unlawfully developed emotional entanglements without the consent and in most cases knowledge of the civilized creates a delusional relationship that they manipulate to continue with their demonic persecutory practices. The delusional state of mind of the uncivilized psychopaths generated from the wrong interpretation of the constitution that makes them believe that they can invade unlawfully the privacy of the civilized is what gives the civilized dominion over them, when the constitution is interpreted correctly.

The persecuted state of the civilized and the horrific state of the world and vulnerable confirms that the uncivilized collectively are responsible and are psychopaths. A lot of things that are happening and that have happened in the past will not have been possible or will not be possible without the collective participation of the uncivilized given the nature of the supernatural constitution. Given the magnitude of their abominations, to create a more sadistic effect, the uncivilized have collectively insisted on the victims of their vicious actions to trust their judgements. This appears to be their sadistic interpretation of having faith. These uncivilized psychopaths are playing Russian roulette with the health and safety of those different from them. This includes the unlawful alterations or the deliberate misinterpretations of the real constitution regarding the real civil rights of the civilized. This also includes the unlawful practicing of supernaturalism, they try to justify because of deliberately created problems resulting from their interference with nature or the natural order of things. The unlawful attempts by the conspiracy of the uncivilized to compromise the constitutional authority of Lord Adam and the civil constitution, have only served to strengthen the constitutional authority of Lord Adam and the civil constitution. They have unlawfully attempted to make the civilized dependent on the unhealthy exposure to supernaturalism or poison by undermining the little protection the legislations give the civilized, legislations they enacted while pretending to be civilized, they sabotage any process involving the civilized exercising any legal rights not for any good intentions but to make life worse for the civilized unlawfully. Given the destructive pattern of behaviour of the uncivilized constitution from the beginning of time, any pretence involving a false show of correcting problems they are responsible for that involves mental or physical harm to the civil constitution and the vulnerable will be interpreted as punishable attacks. The destructive pattern of behaviour of the uncivilized constitution is very predictable, not a surprise, you do not have to be supernatural to know their preferred option in any situation. This is why there are strict guidelines in the constitution regarding contact with civilized and behaviour in a civilized society. The education meant for everyone is to ask yourselves what you are gaining from a particular type of system of government. Are you gaining life or death, war or peace, sickness or good health, independence or dependency, slavery or freedom?

The media has always used the success of the entertainment industry, films, music to promote their agendas. They do this by using actors and actresses and musicians to promote politics and different lawless activities. The political demonic lawless agenda has been expanded by the unlawful alteration of the images in films and the voices in music, making them supernatural or lawless.

The uncivilized have conspired by misinformation, deliberate misinterpretation of the constitution to create the false impression that they are gods and angels that the vulnerable including the civilized should feel privileged or honoured to be abused, humiliated or persecuted by them. This includes interpreting attacks as help (the unlawful invasion of privacy that they try to justify because of the unlawful system of government they are responsible for). It is similar to slavery, when a slave master wants a slave to be grateful to be a slave and to feel honoured and privileged to be abused by the slave master.

When uncivilized psychopaths try to threaten or intimidate the civilized by misusing their supernatural powers and senses in order to continue with their unlawful practices, it is similar to using gasoline to try to put out fire. The uncivilized psychopaths want the vulnerable including the civilized to live our lives in constant fear that they can kill you anytime they want, make you ill anytime they want, make you destitute anytime they want unlawfully. They like to have this type of power over you. This means that any interest from a supernatural is toxic. Given the unlawful horrific unprovoked attacks on the civilized by the uncivilized, it will be reasonable for the civilized to never want to have contact with the uncivilized. There are no requirements in both the legislations and the real constitution that permits contact with the uncivilized. The legislations do not recognize the altered state of television, radio, films and music. The real constitution will consider any unlawful direct or indirect supernatural contact with the civilized a serious attack. The uncivilized have taken away the little protection the legislations provide, although these United Kingdom legislations are not the real laws from the real constitution, their protection has been taken away not for the better but to make life even more unbearable for the civilized. They now want everything to be dependent on supernaturalism which is unlawful and unhealthy. The civilized now have to unlawfully be dependent on the mood swing of our persecutors, the uncivilized psychopaths. This requires the civilized and the vulnerable to do the impossible and pretend to like your persecutors before you can have access to these United Kingdom basic legal rights provided by these legislations.

This is worse than slavery for the persecuted. If you like watching films your rights are now dependent on the mood swing of illegally altered supernatural images on screen, the supernatural unlawful images on screen. This helps feed the power tripping nature of the uncivilized constitution at the expense of the mental and physical wellbeing of the civilized constitution. They have developed a way to make the lives of the vulnerable including the civilized revolve around constant abuse, by sabotage, altering our interests, so that if you continue with them it will be similar to eating the forbidden fruit in the Garden of Eden. The differences are meant to be permanent with the proper checks and balances in place to provide peace and security. Unfortunately the uncivilized will continue to be a plague in a civilized society and to the civilized, which will require the final safety measure invoked, the civilized can survive without the uncivilized. Lord Adam was created with the intention to live happily without contact with the uncivilized.

Given the toxic pattern of behaviour of the uncivilized, to effect change you do not take away the little protection the legislations in a lawless system provides, you change the lawless system, otherwise their actions will be construed as deliberate attacks on the civilized.

It is very strange but part of the sadistic nature of the uncivilized constitution, when they try to provide solutions supernaturally for a preventable problem they plan to introduce into the lives of the civilized as if helping. These are very severe unlawful attacks on the civilized.

I am a forty one years old civilized man whose life revolves around constant abuse and disrespect from the uncivilized collectively, the uncivilized of all ages in their attempts to protect a lie about their supernatural constitutions, a lie that wreaks havoc on the world. In an attempt to protect this lie I was diagnosed over ten years ago as suffering from a severe mental disorder that is permanent. They said it was because they are not uncivilized with supernatural powers and senses as I claimed, I was hallucinating. This action put a hold on my plans for my life, because I was convinced that my experiences were real and not hallucinations, I had to learn like a child trying to walk for the first time given the new reality they collectively concealed from me all my life. With this new reality I am aware that there are things I see the uncivilized do while pretending to be civilized that I dare not do because it will have a harmful effect on me given the differences. When you are learning as a young person your surroundings influence your development, when you see people pretending to be civilized like you doing things, you believe it is alright to do the same things. The differences mean that I cannot do most of the things they do because it will have a different effect on me. You cannot leave your life in the hands of those with this type of behavioural problems. You cannot leave your future life plans to their judgements. Without being truthful about the differences they have said instead that I am severely mentally impaired of intelligence for social functioning. I see this as a compliment because the social functioning out there is lawless. The problem is that things have to be explained to the civilized properly in a civilized manner. Whether I agree with the disability or not it is permanent and I am as a British citizen entitled to disability benefits. They have never given full payments meant for this disability in my case. Every time I ask why, they tell me that there are others going through the same problems. Their definition of others is the uncivilized that are different from me. I always experience a strange type of hostility from any contact with a supernatural. It must be an uncivilized type of guilty conscience. I now understand that hostility is how they socialize which is incompatible with the civilized constitution. The problem for me is that they always want to initiate unnecessary hostile contact. They try to force these hostile contacts by exploiting your need for money and by exploiting your interests. I experience this unhealthy unprovoked hostility from the police and those that are meant to be responsible for the welfare

of the disabled, so I have learnt to do things myself because I find contact with them unhealthy. They delude themselves into thinking that if I am not behaving hysterically when I have contact with them, that I like them. That is not the case. There must be a health and safety reason why these legislations that governs policing and the care of the disabled do not recognize the uncivilized constitution. This means that acting under these legislations is unlawful if of an uncivilized constitution. This also means that they are not allowed contact with the civil constitution under these legislations. The civilized should not be blamed because it is a revelation that they the uncivilized are doing something wrong. My only experience of the uncivilized constitution is that they are extremely unpleasant and extremely abusive.

The educational value of the problems associated with governing when the uncivilized pretend to be civilized evidenced in the composition of the British parliament and around the world is the importance and role of the civil constitution and a properly constituted government.

Once you are diagnosed with a permanent severe mental disorder the application process is normally a one off process. But because of the toxic unwanted interest in my case they want the process to be on-going for the purposes of hostile abusive contact with uncivilized psychopaths. It is normally a one off process with regard to the disabled because of the distressing effects of an application process. A recent development regarding disability social security benefits is as a consequence of being stalked unlawfully by the uncivilized. I had to leave a doctor's surgery I was registered with for over ten years because of being stalked unlawfully supernaturally by them. My entitlements to social security benefits are not dependent on being registered with a doctor's surgery because the disability has been confirmed as permanent, no cure. The doctor patient relationship is an unlawful social activity. You are made ill supernaturally in order to initiate contact with the uncivilized to cater to their sadistic nature. The doctor patient relationship is an unlawful social activity created for the uncivilized.

If I am telling the truth about the differences which means that I am not hallucinating then I should be in receipt of a salary of about £500,000 per annum as a law lord. So there is nothing to gain for me to be in receipt of disability benefits.

There is a tax in the United Kingdom called the council tax, it was originally known as the poll tax. There are certain groups of people exempt from paying this tax. There is an exemption from this tax for the severely mentally impaired. You can only be exempt from this tax for severe mental impairment if your disability has been determined to be permanent. It is a one off process. Because of the need to create activities for the uncivilized they are trying to make the process a continuous one at the expense of the health of the disabled. When you are identified as disabled the legislations give a degree of protection from some activities. In my case it gives me some protection from the uncivilized pretending to be civilized and causing me serious mental harm.

A social activity for the uncivilized is misusing their supernatural powers and senses to make fools of the civilized unlawfully.

The problem the uncivilized experience with the limited protection disability benefits provides for the civilized is exposing the truth that the civilized will not want to have anything to do with them given the opportunity. This is why they are willing to cripple the civilized financially to hide the truth. A supernatural that develops an unwanted emotional entanglement with the civilized becomes a traitor. The uncivilized have the god complex characteristic that will make them want to interfere

with you or your plans supernaturally without your consent or without an explanation. They will rather opt to interfere with you supernaturally than change a lawless system that will guarantee the independence of the civil constitution. The independence of the civil constitution is important in a civilized society because it is a measure of how civilized a society is. It is cowardice and bias to pick on the victims of a lawless system instead of changing a lawless system to a lawful one.
The uncivilized are correct when they insist that cheating in an examination means that you are a fraud and as consequence you are not intelligent. The uncivilized constitution with their supernatural powers and senses make them natural cheaters. This means that the uncivilized are not as smart or intelligent as they think they are. This is evident when they go over the top pretending to civilized, especially to the civilized.
The lawless system in the world makes it unsafe for the civilized or vulnerable to go out or to have contact with the uncivilized. This is similar to the problems wild animals experience; the weak animals are food for the stronger animals. It is easy for the uncivilized to make a risk assessment of the effects of the lawless system on the civilized and the vulnerable and conclude that it is not that bad or it is an acceptable risk. The lawless system does not have the same effect on the uncivilized as it has on the civilized. Their uncivilized constitution makes them blind to real lawlessness and its effects that is why they are not allowed to govern or to make rules.
The only way the uncivilized can get the attention of the civilized when you do not know them or cannot see them is to harm you mentally or physically by touching you supernaturally.
When I try to watch a film or listen to music the unlawful supernatural images or voices start getting personal with me in indirect ways, as in the fictional film the game. They always try to put my life, health and financial security on the line, so every time I try to do what I normally do, because of the unlawful alterations to them it is as if I am being drawn into a type of Russian roulette. As a consequence I cannot relax when I watch a film or listen to music which is the opposite effect of their intended purpose. They always power trip as their supernatural life version that surrounds me when I go out which is rare because of the harmful effects of supernaturalism on the civilized.
The uncivilized should understand when misusing their supernatural powers and senses to instigate or plan supernatural lawless social events or problems in my life that they are facilitating their own self-destruction, which is suicide proportionate to the supernatural constitution. The supernatural plans the life of the civilized like a lower life form that should not have a life similar to the life of a weak wild animal that is not allowed to have a life by a stronger animal that sees it as food. The civilized are unlawfully not allowed to have a life, like go on holiday, buy a new car, and have access to our real entitlements etc. without worrying about the financial consequences.
When your interests or hobbies have been unlawfully supernaturally altered to force unwanted contact with the uncivilized the problematic supernatural characteristics of power tripping becomes evident and a very serious problem, when you are outside the uncivilized cater to the power tripping interference of the supernatural images or voices in films and music, this is a subtle conspiracy by the uncivilized to dominate the civilized inside your home and outside. They want your life to dependent on a very unhealthy and unlawful phenomenon supernaturalism. This is similar in principle to what happened to the fictional character in the film the game, every relationship he had were exploited to harm him physically and mentally. The difference in my case is that supernaturalism is not a game but an unlawful attack on the civilized.
The madness of the uncivilized is everywhere, reality television shows have turned companionship into what should be seen as an abomination it encourages going outside the boundaries of sanity to

establish a relationship. The same madness has entered the process of getting your social security entitlements, it is now show based to cater to the need of the uncivilized for a lawless social activity exploiting its need for their sadistic pleasure. People do not give up on life because they do not like it, they give up because the toxic interest in their lives from the uncivilized. Given my experiences as someone of a civilized constitution Lord Adam could have lost the will to live because of the toxic interest in him from the uncivilized. The uncivilized plan the lives of the civilized as if writing a script for a movie, regardless of the mental and physical harm to the civilized. They think that because they can take things apart and put them back together they can take any risk with the mental and physical wellbeing of the civilized.

When the uncivilized pretend unlawfully to be civilized and try to deny the civilized our constitutional or civil rights, and try to establish a relationship with the civilized outside the guidelines of the real constitution, it makes them traitors like the character played by Sean Penn in the film the game and Peter and Judas in the bible. This is why the uncivilized try to establish personal relationships with civilized, when that fails, they try to establish an unlawful supernatural relationship with the civilized by force for the same treacherous purposes.

As a real law lord because of my civilized constitution, after careful investigation and being subjected to similar experiences, I must conclude that Lord Adam was innocent of the charges against him as he had no supernatural powers and senses. His constitutional rights guaranteed him peace and security from harm, including security from harmful alteration of his then civilized constitution. So it will be reasonable to conclude that he was unlawfully setup by the uncivilized with the misuse of their supernatural powers and senses. As a fictional character Shylock Holmes says as he investigates a crime, if you eliminate the impossible whatever remains however improbable must be the truth. Heaven means haven or shelter which the law represents, the civil constitution is a living representation of the law. It is correct to say that the civilized are collectively severely mentally impaired of intelligence for the current lawless social functioning in the world at present.

Once I graduated from university in 1995 with an honours degree in law, I made every reasonable effort to join the Metropolitan police force and Thames valley police force, my efforts included a complaint to the then prime minister the Right honourable Anthony Blair when my application to Thames valley police was declined after being made to go to Thames valley police force for two days for the second stage of their selection process. You need to note that I still was not aware at the time of the differences in their uncivilized constitutions and my civilized constitution. I was not aware at the time that I am a law lord (commissioner of police and a Supreme Court judge).

The law or constitution in principle for purposes of law and order bears a grudge; you must be punished for crimes you commit.

As a consequence of the irrational behaviour associated with the uncivilized constitution, issues of keeping the peace and the administration of justice must be done properly by a legally commissioned police force. A legal police force and a proper system in place for the administration of justice can only be commissioned or legally authorized by law lords, the civilized. This is an essential requirement in the constitution.

A civil lawful administration does not require personal relationships with anyone to guarantee your individual rights unlike a supernatural lawless political administration requiring you to pretend to like toxins the uncivilized when they are being demonically abusive.

The current unlawful interpretation of the constitution or the Christian principles which unlawfully encourages supernaturalism is responsible for lawlessness or hell on earth. This unlawful interpretation implies that the uncivilized are above the law and can do no wrong. Even the uncivilized see a serious problem with this unlawful interpretation.

Life will be impossible for the uncivilized and the civilized and the vulnerable with this unlawful interpretation of the constitution. The correct interpretation of the constitution identifies the civilized as law lords or system lords and the uncivilized are meant to aspire to the natural qualities of the civil constitution. This means that the uncivilized should learn how to be supernatural within the guidelines of the real constitution. You cannot be a constitution you are not.

With regard to the unlawful alterations to television, radio, music and films, which have made the voices and images supernatural apart from the unhealthy effect on the civilized watching or listening, I have no idea of its true effects on the supernatural images or voices but I am aware that according to the real constitution if they are life rather than recorded images or voices they should not be created for this purpose. The original concept of people going to a location to film for a movie or record for music is the legal healthier option for actors, musicians, and a civilized audience. When the uncivilized misuse their supernatural powers and senses collectively to poison the air, and the civilized have no choice but to breathe the air in its poisoned state, you cannot blame the civilized for breathing the air as if willingly eating a forbidden fruit.

I do not see how all the oranges on this planet can satisfy the need of a day's consumption of orange juice in a country like the United Kingdom, which will suggest a type of replication similar to the replication technology in the science fiction drama series star trek. If this is the case then milk is alright to drink or eat, the only problem I had with milk was what I thought was the method of manufacture involving the abuse of animals. The constitution clearly mentions the possibility of the constant replication of milk and honey without the abuse of animals, with its mention of a land flowing with milk and honey.

The uncivilized psychopaths think that the unlawful circumstance that led to the downfall of Lord Adam gives them permission to undermine or compromise the sacred civil constitution rather than it being a lesson of what they should not do because of the consequences of lawlessness.

The admission of the legal requirement for clarity with regard to the real rights and privileges of the civilized rather than the unlawful confusing practice of riddles by the uncivilized will be an admission of guilt and culpability for the unlawful persecuted state of the civilized.

Role play or acting is based on the principle that the parties involved must consent beforehand and know what will happen beforehand like a movie script, it has to be safe for the parties involved. This is a description of the way the uncivilized live amongst themselves or interact because of their supernatural powers and senses. The problem with trying to involve the civilized in this way of life acting or role play is that we do not have supernatural powers and senses and go into any situation in good faith not knowing beforehand what will happen. The uncivilized need to be aware when making plans with the lives of the civilized in role play situations that we cannot consent to it regardless of appearances. The constitution's requirement for the female companions of a civilized man to honour and obey him is for security purposes to eliminate unnecessary dramatics. It is based on this principle that communications that will normally be considered as requests, applications or invitations etcetera should be taken as orders or instructions from the civilized for security purposes. The concept in the science fiction drama series star trek with regard to the replication technology is good, it is an established way of production outlined in the real constitution or bible, the problem is what you replicate and how you replicate. An example is the replication of eggs because it is similar to replicating an unborn child because you have a taste for unborn children. In my capacity as a law

lord I believe that the replication of fish is unlawful. To replicate bread is alright.
When the uncivilized pretend to be civilized with the intention of deceiving the civilized and

advocating a life style that is harmful to the real civilized, they are unlawfully indirectly cursing the civilized. Examples of the deception are, the unlawful life span which includes death, ageing and illnesses, the unlawful work concept, misleading practices of eating meat, fish and eggs, being married with children, the worshipping of the uncivilized in mosques , synagogues and churches etcetera.

The media is responsible for maintaining the false impressions created about the civil constitution which is still on-going, insisting that the civil constitution is capable of criminal behaviour. This is achieved by the creation of demonic rules which suggests that it is possible for the civil constitution to commit a crime or to sin contrary to guidance of the real constitution. This is further achieved by unlawfully altering the constitutional living conditions meant for the civil constitution and the redefining of what constitutes a crime in order to undermine the constitutional authority of the civil constitution similar in principle to what happened in the film trading places.

## 5. Author's notes

This is my eighth non-fiction book about the law. It is about the correct identification, interpretation and application of the constitution of this planet. The correct identification of the constitution, which is the Christian principles or the civil constitution of man, exposes the direct and indirect misuse of supernatural powers and senses by the uncivilized that undermines international peace and security which creates lawlessness. The uncivilized, those with supernatural powers and senses thrive on hostile chaotic living conditions, hostile relationships, as a consequence aspire to create hell on earth to cater to their uncivilized natures contrary to the constitution and at the expense of the mental and physical wellbeing of the vulnerable including the civilized, those without supernatural powers and senses.

# THE MEDIA

## 6. Author's biography

My name is Lord Loveday Ememe. I am of a civilized nature, which my surname indicates for some reason. I am a graduate of an Anglican seminary school, which is a real police academy. I also graduated from the University of East London with an honours degree in law.

## Bibliography

THE BIBLE.

www.ingramcontent.com/pod-product-compliance
Lightning Source LLC
Chambersburg PA
CBHW072253170526
45158CB00003BA/1068